Penshurst Place

I hope you wi .... ing about this old .... garden. Penshurst reveals its secrets reluctantly as befits a house which has for so long been subject to the vicissitudes of history and social change. My family have been privileged to be in continuous occupation of the house for 450 years, since Edward VI granted the estate to Sir William Sidney in 1552.

Explore the gardens, which date from the first Elizabethan age, when Sir Henry Sidney laid out his formal garden. Today the levels he formed underpin a series of garden rooms fashioned by yew hedges planted in the 19th century. Both house and garden belong to each other and have done so for many centuries.

This guide has been prepared to help unravel the mysteries of Penshurst and the part owners have played in its history. It is not intended as a room-by-room guide, for which you will find more detailed information in each of the state rooms. The information on the garden is intended to supplement your own interpretation and is a fitting memorial to my father who lavished 45 years of care upon it and the house. This work must be continuous if the house is to survive another 450 years.

All of us who live and work at Penshurst hope you will enjoy your visit to us and that this guide will act as a companion not only here but also as a reminder of your visit after you have returned home.

De L'Isle

Photo: David Sellman

Contents

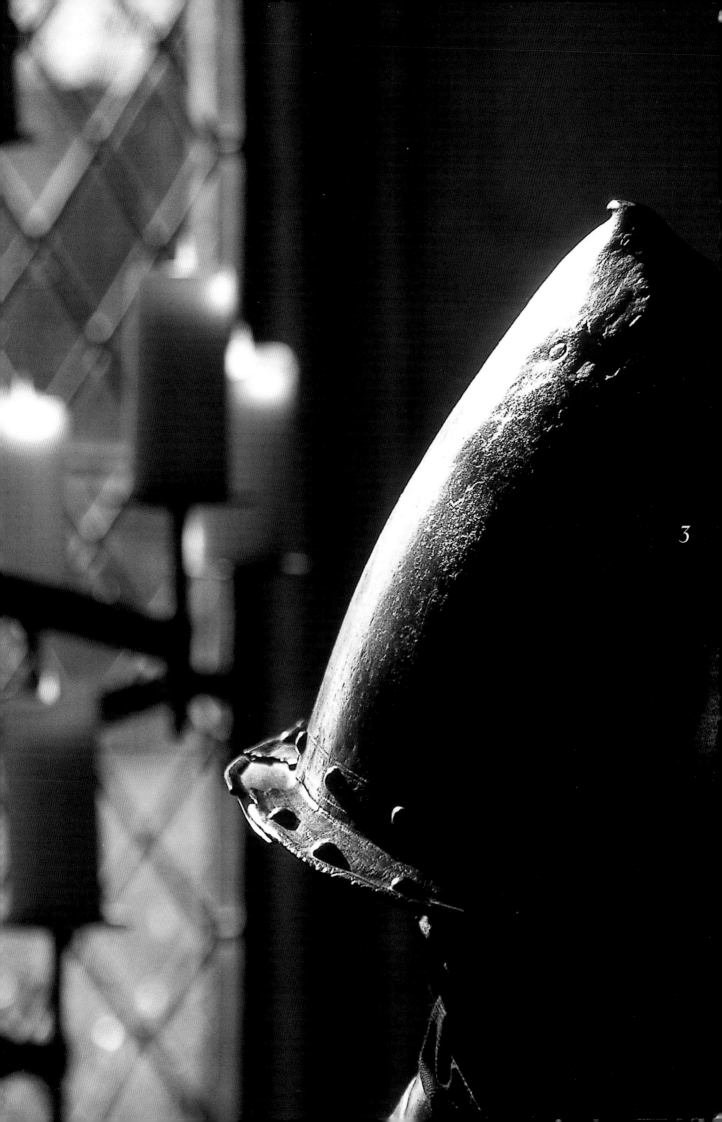

3

Photo: David Markson

Photo: David Sellman

Photo: Christopher Simon-Sykes

Photo: David Markson

Photo: David Markson

Introduction

Penshurst Place - house and home

Penshurst Place invites superlatives. The manor house that lies at its heart is the finest and most complete example in England of 14th century domestic architecture.

The great hall, with its vast, sunlit, arching chestnut roof and rare octagonal hearth has been described as one of the world's grandest rooms. The 6 metre (20ft) long 15th century trestle tables it contains are unique. The gardens, too, with origins as old as those of the house, are special. They retain the Elizabethan formal framework now seldom found at other great houses, where 18th century improvers destroyed the ancient structures. Today, the garden rooms, bounded by formal yews, delight with their surprises. It has been described as the best cared-for formal garden in England.

The owners of Penshurst have also played their part in its greatness. Through them the house is deeply embedded in English history. It has been the residence of kings and dukes and of the great soldier, courtier and poet, Sir Philip Sidney. He, in turn, is just one of the Sidneys for whom Penshurst has been home for 450 years. For Penshurst is, and always has been, a home and not just a house. Centuries of visitors have found it thus - those who come today and those also of the past, not least among them the poet Ben Jonson who wrote:

Now, Penshurst, they that will proportion thee
With other edifices, when they see
Those proud, ambitious heaps, and nothing else,
May say, their lords have built, but thy lord dwells.

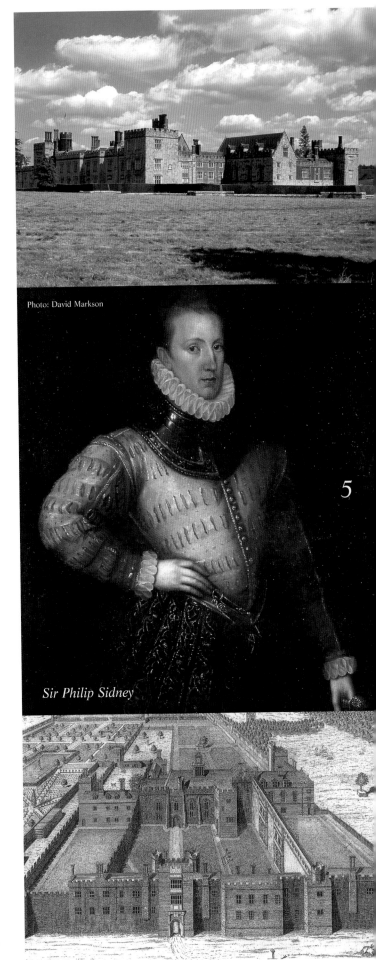

Photo: David Markson

Sir Philip Sidney

5

Mediaeval magnificence

1341-1521

All these things are of the past, and of the fashion of the past which can never be revived and we love the spot which makes us feel it.

Visit to Penshurst, Anon 1838

6

Nobody in 14th century England, with the possible exception of the Archbishop of Canterbury and a few noblemen, had a grander hall than Sir John de Pulteney. But then few commoners had Pulteney's social standing or, more importantly, the kind of money needed to construct such a magnificent edifice. The hall was enormous, measuring 62 by 39ft (19 by 12m) and soaring 60ft (18.3m) to the vast chestnut span of the roof. Life-size carved wooden figures supported the great arched braces of the roof.

Windows ingeniously placed high in the gables dispelled the gloom, so that the craftsmanship would always be properly seen - and properly admired.

It was 1341 when the masons and carpenters - among the best of their time - at last downed tools and left the owner of the house to his first quiet tour. It was in the typical mediaeval manor style, two wings joined by a great central hall, which he knew would be hard to beat for size and splendour.

That inspection of this magnificent monument to his achievements would surely have been sweeter still, though, had he known that the hall would remain, at the beginning of the 21st century, the finest example of its time. The intervening years have seen other buildings grow up around it, but the hall is the most important of them all. Described by John Julius Norwich as one of the grandest rooms in the world, Pulteney's hall, now known as the Baron's Hall, is the very heart of Penshurst Place. Pulteney's money came from London. He was a member of the Draper's Company and dealt in wine as well as wool. At one stage he provided food for the King's troops and, finding favour in high places, supplied the royal household too.

He also lent money, most notably to the King, Edward III, for hostilities with France. By the late 1330s the Crown was in debt to him for many thousands of pounds. Not only was he a rich merchant but was also elected Mayor of London four times and owned two large town houses. But he wanted a country establishment too, where he could hunt. In 1338 he bought the Penshurst estate - 4000 acres within half a day's hard riding back to the centre of affairs in London. Little is known of Penshurst prior to that date.
Sir Stephen de Penchester, buried in Penshurst Church, owned the estate in the 13th century. The licence for the first rector at Penshurst church was granted in 1170 by Archbishop Thomas à Becket just before he was murdered in Canterbury Cathedral.

Nor do we know who it was that Sir John de Pulteney chose to build the house on the site some half a century after Penchester's death. However, the quality of the work indicates that this wealthy merchant and financier used the best of his day. The architect has been suggested as William de Ramsey III, one of King Edward III's masons, while the King's carpenter, William Hurley, to whom Ely cathedral's magnificent lantern is due, might well have constructed the hall roof, its crowning glory. Perhaps the King's large debts to Sir John de Pulteney were partly offset by the loan of his own architect and carpenter.

Sir John de Pulteney lent money to Edward III, shown here being crowned, to finance his hostilities with France.

Life-size wooden figures support the roof in the Baron's Hall. They are satirical representations of peasants and workers at the manor.

Edward I appointed his faithful servant Sir Stephen de Penchester Sheriff of Kent and warden of the Cinque Ports.

7

The Baron's Hall roof showing the original mediaeval beams of the ceiling.

The architect chose chestnut for his design, stronger but lighter than the usual oak. Kingposts rest on collar beams, held in place by huge arched supports. These culminate at their bases in 10 life-size wooden figures at the wall; satirical representations of peasants and workers at the manor.

The house is built of local sandstone. Its natural rich brown streaks are enhanced by the use of different-sized blocks to give a random, mottled effect. Over the windows, which reach almost to the ground, the stone's grain precisely follows the line of the arch blocks, skilfully adding visual emphasis.

In the centre of the floor, which was originally earth strewn with rushes, is a unique octagonal hearth. From here, smoke would have risen to escape

The Long Gallery and Buckingham Building from the Italian Garden.

through a vent in the roof. The hall was far too large to have been heated by a fireplace and chimney. The vent was later covered by a lantern, though the 19th century saw both vent blocked and lantern removed. At one end of the hall the buttery and pantry lie on either side of a passage which led to the mediaeval kitchens, demolished in the 19th century. At the other end are the undercroft and, above it, Pulteney's solar - now the state dining room.

In 1341 Pulteney was granted a licence to crenellate the house, yet the battlements were intended only to impress. Some 40 years after his death from bubonic plague in 1349, however, a similar licence was given to the then owner of Penshurst for fortifications that were not only a good deal more spectacular but which were amply prepared for a fight.

With vivid memories of the violence of the Peasants' Revolt in 1380 and the threat of foreign invasion as his spur, Sir John Devereux set about enclosing his manor with a massive 375 x 280ft (114 x 85m) system of crenellated curtain walls and turrets, so creating a defended manor house. It must have been a formidable sight, rare in its grand scale and strict symmetry, and cutting a harsh swathe into the green folds of the Kentish landscape. Today the wounds have healed. The sweep of Penshurst's parkland gives few clues as to where the great stone enclosure ran.

Look again, though, and the ghost of the pattern is there. The additions which centuries of successive owners made to the house point like fingers to the old lines of the walls and their towers. The curious shape of Penshurst Place today, with its long arms reaching out far from the centre, is, in its way, a great signpost to the place of Devereux's defences.

8

Two 18th century engravings by Kip and Vertue show a strong tower rising from each corner of the walls, while midway along each sits a smaller tower. One of these lesser towers is all that is now left. Known as the Garden Tower, it stands alone to guard the south of the house, attached to a fragment of the curtain wall.

Sixty years after Pulteney's death, Penshurst was in the hands of King Henry IV's third son, John, Duke of Bedford. To him is attributed the second hall, known as the Buckingham Building, set at one corner of Pulteney's house. His emblems, the falcon and the ibex, adorn its gables. It is thought to date from around 1430, a time when domestic buildings of the splendour of the Buckingham Building were rare. Its principal apartments are Queen Elizabeth's Room and the Tapestry Room. After Bedford's death, Penshurst became the property of his younger brother, Humphrey, Duke of Gloucester, founder of Oxford's Bodleian Library. It then went to Humphrey Stafford, Ist Duke of Buckingham. He was the first of three of that title to own the estate. In 1519, Henry VIII arrived at Penshurst as the 3rd Duke of Buckingham's guest - an event on

Henry Stafford, the 2nd Duke of Buckingham, was beheaded in 1483 by Richard III, for high treason. Henry joined the unsuccessful plot to put the Earl of Richmond on the throne.

A mythical ancestor, 1151. Ostensibly a royal grant of the Manor of Sutton, Surrey to William de Sidne, Kt. Sir William is however a fictitious character as the deed is a forgery by Robert Cooke, a 16th century King of Arms, who wished to magnify the early importance of the family.

which the duke saw fit to lavish the staggering sum of £2,500 - £1.2 million in today's money. Such extravagance could hardly fail to have made an impression, but just two years later any impressions Henry had of Buckingham were far from good. Henry had no male heir and saw Buckingham as a threat. Known as "the proud Buckingham", he had quite a strong claim to the throne himself. Thus Henry found an excuse to have him tried for treason and beheaded. Traitor's estates became forfeit to the Crown. So the two noble halls, the great walls and turrets, the gardens of fruit and vegetables and the woods and pastures of Penshurst were looked after by the brother of Anne Boleyn, while Henry stayed at Penshurst and courted Anne in the nearby castle of Hever. It was left to Henry's successor, Edward VI, to settle the fate of Penshurst. He made a special gift of it to a member of the family who still own it to this day, and who, in the past 450 years, have twice rescued it from decay.

9

To my faithful servant, Penshurst
1521 - 1743

Tread,

As with a pilgrim's reverential thoughts,

The groves of Penshurst. Sidney here was born

Sidney, than whom no gentler, braver man

Its own delightful genius ever feigned

Southey

Unlike so many great houses, Penshurst Place does not stand out as being representative of one particular style of English furnishing or building. Instead, each century since the 14th has made its own contribution. Architecturally, it combines the work of at least eight periods. Its successive owners add to its distinction. Those who have created Penshurst have contributed to English history and culture to an extent which few other houses can rival in an unbroken line, and down the years include names feted in poetry, politics, chivalry and honour. Yet it is not only its place in the nation's heritage which makes Penshurst special. For nearly 450 years it has been and remains the much-loved home of just one family, including the current generations now living and working here.

After Buckingham's violent end at the hands of Henry VIII, the Penshurst estate remained Crown land for some 30 years. But Henry's successor, Edward VI, wanted to reward the services of the man who was both his tutor and steward of his household, and saw Penshurst as a fitting gift. So it was that the house and its lands came into the hands of **Sir William Sidney** in 1552. He had not long to live, however,

and two years later the estate passed to his son Sir Henry.

Sir Henry Sidney had spent his childhood at court as the constant companion of the young Prince Edward. On his accession as Edward VI, Sir Henry remained his closest friend. Legend has it that Edward died in his arms. Sir Henry also became one of the most faithful servants of Queen Elizabeth I, assuming responsibility in Ireland for over 20 years, first as vice-treasurer of the Irish

Robert Dudley, Earl of Leicester, was a strong candidate for Queen Elizabeth I's hand. She refused his offer of marriage, but he continued to enjoy her favour until his death in 1588.

Council and later as Lord Deputy. He was made a Knight of the Garter in 1564, yet generally received little thanks for his services, and equally little reward. By 1583 he was £5,000 in debt, complaining that he had not "*so much land as would graze a mutton*". He had even turned down a barony, feeling financially unable to support the rank.

On the other hand, Henry was a survivor in the dangerous family politics of the time. His wife, Mary, was a Dudley and sister to Guildford. Guildford's wife was Lady Jane Grey, queen for just nine days before she and Guildford were sent to the scaffold for scheming to exclude Henry VIII's daughter, the eventual Bloody Queen Mary, from the throne. Guildford's father - and Henry Sidney's father-in-law - John, Duke of Northumberland was also executed, whilst his sons Ambrose Dudley, Earl of Warwick and Robert Dudley, Earl of Leicester - Henry Sidney's brothers-in-law - were consigned to the Tower.

11

This painting shows Queen Elizabeth I dancing 'La Volta' with Robert Dudley the Earl of Leicester. The brother of the King of France, Charles, is in the foreground with his arm around a lady whilst Sir Philip Sidney (by the fireplace), is pointing this indiscretion out to Leicester. Charles was supposed to have been courting the Queen at the time.

But Henry and his wife escaped implication in the plot. Not for the last time was Penshurst saved by the astuteness of its owners. In due course Robert Dudley became Queen Elizabeth I's great favourite whilst his sister Mary and her husband continued to serve their queen faithfully. Mary's face bore the scars of her service, for whilst nursing Queen Elizabeth through smallpox she contracted the dreaded illness herself. Her face was left so disfigured that she felt obliged to wear a mask in public.

Scant reward at court did not prevent Henry making substantial additions to his house at Penshurst - and with an unusual care to preserve its mediaeval character. One of the key schemes saw three ranges of apartments rise to the north of Pulteney's hall. Here, Henry incorporated one of the earliest classical loggias in England and a new entrance tower. This is known as the King's Tower from the plaque he set on it to commemorate Edward's gift of Penshurst to his father. He also made alterations to the Buckingham Building,

adding an attic storey and dividing the first floor hall into a series of state rooms.

Henry and Mary's first child, born in 1554, was to live only 31 years, but in that short time he came to represent all the qualities and talents to which any Renaissance gentleman could aspire. His is a reputation which persists to this day. **Sir Philip Sidney** remains the personification of virtue, chivalry and nobility.

Below and following pages: Contemporary scroll depicting the mourners at the unprecedented State Funeral of Sir Philip Sidney.

Amongst the mourners are several celebrated personalities of the age including (over the page), Sir Francis Drake.

13

Sir Philip Sidney wounded on the battlefield at Zutphen, 1586.

Sir Francis Drake.

Sir Robert Sidney became Earl of Leicester in 1618, a title previously held by his uncle, Robert Dudley.

Sir Philip Sidney died only a few months after his father, so he never took control of the Penshurst estate. It therefore passed to his brother **Robert**, who did much to further the family status. Within a few weeks of the succession to the throne of King James I in 1603 he was made **Baron Sidney of Penshurst**, thus becoming the first of his family to accept a peerage. He was later elevated to the **Viscountcy of Lisle**, reviving a title previously held by his uncle, the Earl of Warwick, and became a Knight of the Garter in 1616 as had his father 52 years before. The next Sidney to be made a Garter Knight was William 1st Viscount De L'Isle, 352 years later in 1968. The Earldom of Leicester, conferred on Robert in 1618, revived a title previously held by another uncle, Robert Dudley.

Barbara Gamage and her six children. Her hands rest on her two sons, William and Robert, who are dressed in skirts like their sisters, in the fashion of the time.

14

The Sidney funds too started to assume a new dignity. Robert had been heir to both Warwick and Leicester uncles, and in 1582 had married a Welsh heiress, Barbara Gamage. He adored her - and not only for the Glamorganshire property, including coal mines, which she had added to the Sidney estates. *"Sweet Barbara,"* he once wrote to her, *"as you love me do not discomfort yourself, you are one of the greatest joys of my life."* The State Dining room holds a striking conversation piece, painted in 1596 by the elder Gheeraerts, showing Barbara with six of her children. A portrait of her husband Robert hangs to its left. It is Robert whom Penshurst has to thank for the Long Gallery, an addition to the sequence of state rooms. It is unusual in being lit by windows on three sides, and the fine panelling is original. Robert may also have built the range of offices to the east of Pulteney's Hall, which saw the house reach its greatest extent.

A quiet intellectual - Robert Sidney, 2nd Earl of Leicester, became Charles I's ambassador in Paris.

Meanwhile, the family lacked a house in London, an embarrassment which Robert's son and successor determined should be suffered no longer. **The 2nd Earl of Leicester, also Robert**, set about acquiring in the early 1630s a large plot of land near Westminster on which to build a residence to match the Sidney status.

Robert Sidney, 2nd Earl of Leicester, built a large house near Westminster to suit the Sidneys' status. It has long since been pulled down - the only hint of its existence is the address - 'Leicester Square, London'.

15

The portraits of Leicester House now hanging in Penshurst's Tapestry Room show that it did. The mansion was roughly twice the size of Penshurst. Yet financially it was to prove a nightmare, both for the Earl and the Sidneys who followed him. The money could never quite support the magnificence. The mansion was let out, and pulled down less than 100 years after it had been built. No hint of its existence is yielded by the Empire Theatre, now on the site - only by its address, Leicester Square. The original Leicester Square lies quietly in the village of Penshurst, a perfect blend of buildings that date from the 14th to the 19th centuries, creating an entrance to the church through which villagers have come to worship for nearly 900 years.

Sadly, nothing remains of Robert's other great legacy to the Sidneys, the magnificent library which he created at Penshurst. He was a quiet intellectual, and might have been a happier man had he been able to spend all his days among his books. Yet he had a devotion to duty and took an active part in public life, holding a number of diplomatic posts. One of these was as ambassador for King Charles I in Paris, but Robert was a noted Parliamentarian and was to lose the King's confidence; after Charles' execution, Parliament entrusted him with the care of two of the late King's children, Henry Duke of Gloucester and Princess Mary.

Of the 2nd earl's seven children, all three sons, like their father, adopted a radical side in politics. Most noted was Algernon Sidney. Taking his great-uncle Philip as his model, and dubbed *The Porcupine*, he was executed in 1683 for alleged complicity in the *Rye House Plot* against King Charles II.

16

Algernon, the Parliamentarian, was executed by Charles II for his supposed involvement in the Rye House plot.

Henry (brother of Algernon), in a painting by Lely as a young shepherd boy, was one of the leading whigs who invited William of Orange to England to become crowned William III.

The eldest son, Philip, fought with Algernon in the Parliamentary army and sat in Cromwell's House of Lords, while their younger brother, Henry, was among the leading Whigs to arrange the deposition of King James II by inviting to England the Prince of Orange. Henry's reward came in being created Earl of Romney by the King, who then reigned as William III with his consort, Mary.

Meanwhile, one of the sisters, Dorothy, was achieving fame as a great beauty - verified by Van Dyck's portrait of her in the Long Gallery - and has passed into history as the Sacharissa of the love poems of Edmund Waller. Alas, poor Waller, there proved little more than his verse to commend him, and he was duly out-wooed by Lord Spencer, soon to become the 1st Earl of Sunderland. From their union were to descend Sir Winston Churchill and the late Diana, Princess of Wales.

Robert, 2nd Earl of Leicester, was succeeded by another **Philip** as the **3rd Earl of Leicester** in 1677, who was, in turn, followed by his son, **Robert** in 1698. This 4th earl's marriage produced no less than 15 children. Three of the sons succeeded to the earldom, but none produced the heir which would have carried it on to the next generation.

Philip, 5th earl, died childless in 1705. **John**, his brother and successor, remained unmarried, dying in 1737. Thus, it was left to the **7th earl, Jocelyn**, to do his bit for posterity, but he achieved as little distinction in this respect as in the rest of his duties. He led an indecorous life, substantially aiding the dwindling of the Sidney fortune and selling the 2nd earl's great library to help support his pleasures. He chose a wife who indulged in such unsuitable pastimes as entertaining young men in rustic snuggeries; and attending country dances. They never lived together. He produced only one child - an illegitimate daughter.

Thus, when the 7th Earl of Leicester died in 1743, so too did the Leicester earldom.

Dorothy Sidney was famed as a great beauty.

Philip 3rd Earl

Robert 4th Earl

Philip 5th Earl

John 6th Earl

Jocelyn 7th Earl as a child

17

Sir Philip Sidney:

'a rare ornament of his age'

"Even at this great distance Sidney is dazzling," C. S. Lewis said of Sir Philip Sidney. *"He is that rare thing, the aristocrat in whom the aristocratic ideal is really embodied."*

Lewis was writing of English literature of the 16th century, for his subject also stands in the front rank of Elizabethan writers. And while *"the aristocratic ideal"* may be less recognisable to, or appreciated by, a 21st than a 16th century world, Sir Philip's literary genius is not.

Philip was born at Penshurst on November 30th 1554, named after and godson to Philip II of Spain, husband of the then monarch, Queen Mary. Intelligent and politically aware, he was to become a brave soldier, with a deep interest in colonial expansion, and remained free of scandal. Unusually for that time, he spurned field sports, considering them to be the pastime of blood thirsty tyrants. As a patron of the arts, though, he was well known and, being himself a writer, was intent on raising the standards of literature in England. His scholarly leanings showed from an early age. *"Nights and days in ceaseless and related studies he worked upon the anvil of wit, reason and memory, at some harm to his welfare,"* noted an observer of the small boy.

Philip's qualities were not lost on his father Henry, nor on his beloved younger brother Robert. In a letter to Robert, their father urged him to emulate his eldest son: *"Imitate his virtues, exercises, studies, and actions. He is a rare ornament of his age: the very formula that all well-disposed young gentlemen of our court do form also their manners and life by. In truth, I speak it*

A detail from the contemporary funeral scroll, depicting Nicholas Paddy, alias 'Rouge Dragon', carrying Sir Philip Sidney's funeral helm, which can be seen today in the Nether Gallery at Penshurst.

18

19

Mr Tho: Dudley.

Mr Foulke Greuell

Mr Edw Wootto

Mr Edm: Walsingham

Mr Edw: Dyet

without flattery of him, or myself, he hath the most virtues that I ever found in any man."

Yet Philip was no prig. The best-known portrait of him, painted when he was 21 and hanging at Penshurst today, shows him as slender and with the kind of red hair said to go with a fierce temper, which he had. He was also recklessly extravagant, impetuous and inclined to be difficult.

Among Sir Philip Sidney's most celebrated literary works are his *Defence of Poesie* and sonnet sequence *Astrophel and Stella*, in which "Astrophel" is Philip and "Stella" the married Lady Penelope Rich, with whom he is in love.

The prose romance *Arcadia*, written for his sister Mary, Countess of Pembroke, is a work in which, said Virginia Woolf, *"all the seeds of English fiction lie latent"*. His description in it of a great house is thought to be modelled on Penshurst: *"The House itself was built of fair and strong stone, not affecting so much any extraordinary kind of fineness as an honourable representing of a firm stateliness...all more lasting than beautiful; but that consideration of the exceeding lastingness made the eye believe it was exceeding beautiful."*

Philip was dogged throughout his life by ill health. Nonetheless, following his years at Shrewsbury School and Christ Church, Oxford he travelled extensively in Europe, mixing with many of its leading figures, poets and artists. On a later trip overseas, canvassing for support for the formation of a Protestant League of Princes to oppose Catholic powers, he was to meet William, Prince of Orange, on whom Philip made a deep impression. He also spent considerable time at Penshurst and at court, waiting on Elizabeth I. Craving her favour, he presented her with sumptuous gifts –

20

jewels of gold, garnished with diamonds, one *"being a whip [with] cords of small seed pearl"*, another *"like a castle...being a pot to set flowers in"*. Yet the queen remained as niggardly in her rewards to Philip as she had been to his father. Though he was knighted, he was repeatedly denied the chance to play his part in affairs of state or be sent on active service.

At last, however, he gained the queen's reluctant permission to fight for the Protestant cause in the Netherlands in a rebellion against Spain. By September 1586 he was on the field of Zutphen, and there received a musket blast to a leg. Within a month he was dead.

As Philip lay mortally wounded he is said to have noticed a dying soldier eyeing him thirstily as he himself was on the point of taking a drink. Without doing so, he passed the water bottle with the words: *"Thy necessity is yet greater than mine."* As much as his poetry and his reputation, it is a phrase which has become immortalised in the English consciousness.

In February 1587, Sir Philip Sidney was accorded the honour of a state funeral at St Paul's Cathedral. He was the first commoner to receive such a tribute, and it was not to be repeated until the death of Nelson and, later, Sir Winston Churchill, who had Sidney blood in his veins. As if for royalty, mourning was worn by the people who lined the streets to watch Sir Philip's great procession go by. Carried aloft in the cavalcade was his funeral helm surmounted by a porcupine, the Sidney family crest.

The helmet (opposite), can be seen at Penshurst in the Nether Gallery, and portraits of Sir Philip, his father Henry and several of their Dudley relations are together in the Long Gallery.

21

*Sir Philip
Sidney's
funeral helm*
is on display in the Nether Gallery

Battle scars

1745-1945

These are the actions... which make human life what it is, and are the fountains of all the good and evil with which its entire surface is so widely and impartially overspread.

Percy Bysshe Shelley

Jocelyn, 7th Earl of Leicester, had left behind him a rather untidy state of affairs - and a host of people whose burning ambition was to tidy it up. Chief among them were Jocelyn's nieces, **Mary** and **Elizabeth Sidney** - daughters of his brother, Colonel Thomas Sidney. Mary had married Sir Brownlow Sherrard and Elizabeth a Mr William Perry. Jocelyn's only child and illegitimate daughter, Anne, played her part too.

22   For some years leading up to Jocelyn's death, all had been engaged in an expensive wrangle over potential ownership of the Penshurst estate. In the event, Mary and Elizabeth became co-heiresses, but a further dispute saw Penshurst fall into the hands of the Perrys some time around 1744.

Elizabeth Sidney inherited Penshurst after a bitter dispute with her sister Mary.

William Perry possessed money, a penchant for things Italian and a mission to modernise - a combination which was to prove largely unfortunate for the house. Architectural features which had impressed him on his Grand Tour soon started to be reproduced at Penshurst with alarming gusto, and at the expense of some of the earlier work.

For other Perry additions however, the house must be grateful. Along with the many pictures and pieces of furniture he brought from Italy, now comprising an important collection, are three scagliola tables, two matching and one bearing the quarterings of the Sidney family arms, and signed and dated 1752. Perry also acquired a harpsichord, which had belonged to Queen Christina of Sweden, a 16th century instrument held in a case gilded in the rococo manner and mounted on an ornately-carved baroque stand. This can now be seen in Queen Elizabeth's Room, as can a conversation piece of the Perry family; William, Elizabeth and five of their six children,

Not long after it was painted, Perry was certified as a lunatic, unable to govern himself or his property. He ended his days far from the Italianate idyll he had created in the heart of Kent, interred in an asylum. He died there in 1757.

The only one of the Perrys' children to marry, **Elizabeth Jane**, took as her husband **Sir Bysshe Shelley**, an alliance which brought together two families sprung from the Sidneys, for in the late 16th century one John Shelley had married a grand-daughter of William, the first Sidney to own Penshurst.

This marriage also strengthened Penshurst's links with the literary world. Bysshe Shelley's first marriage had produced a son, Sir Timothy Shelley; his son, in turn, was Percy Bysshe Shelley, the poet.

Sir Bysshe Shelley, who married Elizabeth Jane Perry, was also the grandfather of the great poet - Percy Bysshe Shelley.

He was a great admirer of the works of his distant relative, Sir Philip Sidney, and modelled his book *A Defence of Poetry* on Sidney's work. He also, like Sidney, held strong political, moral and religious convictions, and there was a parallel in the deaths of the men too; both died unnaturally, and just before their 32nd birthdays.

Percy Bysshe Shelley's uncle John, the son of Elizabeth Jane and Sir Bysshe Shelley, inherited Penshurst from his grandmother, who outlived her unfortunate husband William Perry by a quarter of a century. John was just a boy, however, and the house soon began to deteriorate. One visitor reported that "the mansion is now deserted; and will probably before another generation passes be known only as a ruin." In the event, though, matters took a decided turn for the better once John had reached maturity and claimed the estate from the negligent

Sir John Shelley-Sidney.

hands of the trustees. Using J. B. Rebecca as his architect, he took on an ambitious programme of restoration, refacing with stone the northern exterior and part of the west front and ordering the redecoration of the private apartments in the north and west ranges. This interior work, in particular, was executed with remarkable skill and sensitivity.

In 1818, **John Shelley** was created **Baronet of Penshurst**, beginning the social revival of the family that had taken 75 years to recover from the depredations of the 7th Earl of Leicester. Meanwhile, he had also been keen to emphasise his Sidney ancestry, and had assumed the name Shelley-Sidney. In due course, his son and heir, Philip, dropped the Shelley cognomen and the family once more became known as Sidney. Sir John Shelley-Sidney's son, **Philip**, consolidated the family's recovery. He married Sophia FitzClarence, the favourite child of King William IV, previously the Duke of Clarence, and his long-time mistress, Mrs Dorothy Jordan.

From top to bottom: Philip Sidney, 1st Baron De L'Isle and Dudley his wife Sophia FitzClarence, the daughter of King William IV and his mistress Mrs Dorothy Jordan.

23

Philip Sidney, 2nd Lord De L'Isle and Dudley 1828-1898.

Philip Sidney, 3rd Lord De L'Isle and Dudley 1853-1922.

24

Algernon Sidney, 4th Lord De L'Isle and Dudley 1854-1945.

William Sidney, 5th Lord De L'Isle and Dudley 1859-1945.

The Solar, or State Dining Room, holds one magnificent legacy of this marriage - a fine dinner service with the Royal Coat of Arms given to them by William IV. Sophia was married from her father's house in London's Berkeley Square, and the royal connection saw Philip, her husband, raised to the peerage. In 1835, 92 years after the Leicester earldom had died out, Philip was created Baron De L'Isle and Dudley.

Philip continued the architectural work at Penshurst, his projects including the building of a stable wing to the east of the King's Tower in 1834. His son **Philip, 2nd Lord De L'Isle and Dudley,** employed George Devey for still more restoration, chief of which was the near-total reconstruction of the Buckingham Building. So sensitive was Devey's handling of this awesome project however, that the path of his progress is all but indiscernible. When rebuilding the dilapidated end wall, for instance, he ensured that each stone was marked as it was removed and put back in its original place - conservation and restoration of a quality for which succeeding generations have been immensely grateful.

Fortunately treated with a good deal less respect were the notorious sash windows installed by William Perry. Out they came. The mediaeval character of the building was restored with the tracery now in place.

The roof of Pulteney's original building, the Baron's Hall, was repaired with tremendous care by **Philip,** the oldest of the 2nd Baron's sons, when he in turn succeeded to the peerage in 1898. Having no sons, his brother, **Algernon,** became **4th Lord De L'Isle** in 1922. He took on the restoration of the Long Gallery. In the process, Perry's prized Venetian window was ousted in favour of mullions, and the floor which Perry had lowered was once more raised. For nearly 50 years Penshurst was kept in a quiet, bachelor fashion. But towards the end of Algernon's life, as the final drama of World War II was being fought out, and Penshurst's future owner was himself a young Major in the Grenadier Guards fighting from France via North Africa and Italy, the RAF intercepted three flying bombs high in the skies over the village. The damage they did was not insubstantial, and in his 90th year Algernon was compelled to move to Ingleby, his Yorkshire estate. He died there the following year, and the fourth brother, **William,** became **5th Lord De L'Isle and Dudley.** He himself had done much to conserve and order the family finances whilst his brothers had held the title, but survived only two months. Thus, in 1945, at the age of 35, Algernon's nephew, **William,** became **the 6th Lord De L'Isle and Dudley.** He might have wished for a less burdensome inheritance.

Rt. Hon. Viscount De L'Isle, VCKG, GCMG, GCBO.

Penshurst Place had been unoccupied for the entire winter of 1944/45, lacking heating and many of the windows had been broken by the *doodlebugs.* Damp had crept through the rooms, attacking the portraits, and rendering their subjects grey and unrecognisable. The roof and battlements had taken a battering, and the interior walls and ceilings were in dire need of redecoration. Under the west lawn, the main drainage pipe had fractured and been washed away, leaving all effluent to pass into the ground.

*Field Marshal Viscount Gort VC, GCB, CBE, DSO**MVO MC father of Jacqueline Vereker, who married William Sidney, later Viscount De L'Isle.*

Nevertheless, William soon brought his wife Jacqueline and their young family to Penshurst. Accompanying them were Uncle Algy's butler, Cole, his chauffeur, Sands, the porter, Hector, and Mrs Sands and Mrs Hector - who were not on speaking terms.

Treasure in trust
1945~

The name of Sidney, is identified in the very staple of our minds with a sense of high principle, magnanimity of sentiment, and generous and heroic devotion to the cause of our country and of man.
Visit to Penshurst, Anon 1838

If in 1945, the great house at Penshurst looked little like a stately home, it had a good deal less to offer as a home for a family. War damage was one thing, but, even worse, those domestic arrangements which had survived were hopelessly outmoded. To compound the problems money was short, and so, too, in the months following the War were food, fuel and building materials.

Life at Penshurst for the 6th Lord De L'Isle and Dudley, his wife and children was confined to a few rooms. What is today the private dining room became their sitting room, and they ate in the room that is now the pantry. Their kitchen was the then Still Room. The family was obliged to remain in these cramped quarters for several years. In time, however, the installation of central heating and modern bathrooms held out the promise of a more comfortable existence, while government war damage insurance provisions saw the start of work to restore the state apartments and their pictures and furniture.

Jacqueline Viscountess De L'Isle.

25

Roofs and windows were also repaired and some of the 19th century stonework in the west front replaced. At the same time, the De L'Isles took up the challenge presented by the wilderness of the garden - a labour which Lord De L'Isle later said had taken 40 years to complete. By Derby Day, June 1947 the house was once more opened to the public, though still bearing much evidence of the previous years' destruction and neglect.

A decade later saw the kitchen moved nearer the dining room and the restoration of the Nether Gallery, involving the removal of the sculleries and larders into which it had been divided in the 19th century, and the raising of the ceiling to its original level. Work on the private apartments, begun by J. B. Rebecca, was also completed.

Towards the end of his life in 1991 Lord De L'Isle recalled a spring day in 1946 spent on the Yorkshire estate he had also inherited from his uncle Algernon. He admitted that he and his wife were then sorely tempted to abandon Kent, with all its looming troubles and responsibilities, and settle in their comfortable stone manor house under the Cleveland hills. Instead, history can record that it is to him that Penshurst Place owes both its rescue from potential ruin and its return to its current splendour.

The resurrection of Penshurst, however, is but one achievement for which this remarkable man will be remembered, for he was to become the most politically prominent member of his family since the 17th century. He was also one of the only three men ever to have held both of the highest orders of gallantry and chivalry - Victoria Cross and Knight of the Garter.

William Sidney was born in 1909 and after Eton obtained a degree in classics and history at Magdalene College, Cambridge. In 1934 he qualified as a chartered accountant. During the Second World War he served as a supplementary reservist with the Grenadier Guards, first in France and Belgium and later in North Africa and Italy where, in 1944, he won the Victoria Cross at Anzio.

Major W.P. Sidney, later 1st Viscount De L'Isle VC KG with his father-in-law FM Viscount Gort VC in 1945.

Recovered from injuries, for the next two years he was MP for Chelsea, before taking his seat in the House of Lords on the death of his father. Sir Winston Churchill appointed him Secretary of State for Air in 1951, an office he held until 1955. In the following year he was created Viscount De L'Isle. From 1961 to 1965 he served as Governor-General of Australia, the last Englishman to hold that high office. On the death in 1965 of Sir Sidney Shelley, he inherited the baronetcy of Castle Goring. In 1968 he became a Knight of the Garter.

William 1st Viscount De L'Isle arriving to become Govenor-General in Australia.

William Sidney, 6th Lord De L'Isle Dudley and his wife Jacqueline.

In 1940 Captain William Sidney, later 6th Lord De L'Isle and Dudley, had married Jacqueline, only daughter of Field Marshal Viscount Gort VC. The two families were already connected through the marriage of his uncle Philip, 3rd Lord De L'Isle to the daughter of the 4th Viscount Gort. Viscountess De L'Isle died in Australia in 1962. Four years later William was married, to Margaret, daughter of Major General Thomas Shoubridge DSO and widow of the 3rd Lord Glanusk DSO.

The 1st Viscount and Viscountess De L'Isle and their young family.

William and Jacqueline's marriage produced five children, Elizabeth, Catherine, Anne, Lucy and the third child and heir, Philip, born just three days after his father inherited Penshurst in 1945. Like his father and maternal grandfather, he served in the Grenadier Guards 1966-1979.

On his succession in 1991 **Philip** made Penshurst his family home, together with his wife Isobel, youngest daughter of Sir Edmund Compton GCB

The christening of 2nd Viscount De L'Isle.

KBE, and their two children, Sophia, born 1983, and Philip, born 1985. The work of restoring the house and development of the gardens continues, as it has done over the last 450 years.

Awarded the MBE in 1977, Philip was Honorary Colonel of the 5th (Volunteer) Battalion Princess of Wales' Royal Regiment from 1992 to 1999. He became a Deputy Lieutenant of Kent in 1996. In the nine years prior to the House of Lords Reform Act 2000 he took an active part in the House of Lords, speaking on defence and the rural economy, the latter subject being not only of broad interest to him but one to which he had much to contribute. As the custodian of a great house in a rural community which, in the 21st century must also be a business if it is to survive, he has a valuable insight into the relationship between the countryside and those whose livelihoods are a part of its structure.

Indeed, the Penshurst Place estate is typical of the decline and resurgence of rural communities in recent years. In 1945 it sustained 13 small farms, employing 39 people. Today, the same acreage supports just one quarter of that number. However, Lord De L'Isle has a keen interest in ensuring the social and economic health of rural communities, and is helping to maintain and create new jobs in other directions.

Philip Sidney, 2nd Viscount De L'Isle and his family.

27

An old cart shed on the estate has been refurbished and converted into a Montessori nursery school catering for 40 children and employing around 10 local people. A range of Victorian farm buildings has been turned into workshops to form the Penshurst Enterprise Centre. To ensure that Penshurst village does not lose its local facilities, the Penshurst estate also now owns and runs the sub-Post Office-cum-shop-cum-petrol station. As a result, Lord De L'Isle is the only peer of the realm to be a sub-postmaster – though customers will not find him behind the counter selling stamps!

Isobel, Viscountess De L'Isle, has taken special responsibility for the gardens and contents of Penshurst. But, inevitably, she also shares with her husband the overall job of maintaining Penshurst Place. The task is not for the faint-hearted, intimidating as it is both in scale and importance. Furniture, pictures, textiles and the house itself need continuous attention and restoration. There are also more mundane matters to be seen to, such as the inevitable loose tiles, burst pipes and rewiring, which involve not only the public areas but the offices and private rooms.

The 2,600-acre estate requires constant care too. Continual, planned replanting of the parkland involves projects such as the recent replacement of an avenue of oaks. And then there is the unplanned work, such as the planting of 10,000 new trees in place of those destroyed in the great storm of 1987.

Such responsibilities are not new. Generations of Sidneys preceding Lord and Lady De L'Isle have understood and accepted them, and have handed them on, as the current incumbents will do in their turn. Nothing less than the devotion of the lives of those to whom the house and its gardens are entrusted is demanded by this national treasure, which is still a family home.

28

Famous visitors to Penshurst

Down the centuries Penshurst has played host to many famous people, crowned heads among them. Such was the attraction of Penshurst that some even turned up uninvited.

In 1519, King Henry VIII was treated to a sumptuous programme of entertainments here, which set back the owner some £2,500 - £1.2 million in today's money. Little good it did him. Two years later, Henry had the hospitable but proud and potentially dangerous 3rd Duke of Buckingham arrested, charged with treason and beheaded.

Henry's son, King Edward VI, was a visitor and so, too, was Edward's sister, Queen Elizabeth I. With her came her favourite, Robert Dudley, Earl of Leicester, and his brother, Ambrose, Earl of Warwick, brothers-in-law to her faithful servant, Sir Henry Sidney. Penshurst was a favourite haunt of the queen. A letter from one of her officials in London to Henry's successor at Penshurst, Sir Robert Sidney, notes: *'I have much a doe to persuade my Lady to come up, she being soe farre in love with sweet Penshurst: and nothing cold have brought her unto yt, but the protestations I made that the parke would be gonne, if she wold not take the paines in your lordships absence to come up and to the Court'.*

Queen Elizabeth I visited Penshurst with her favourite suitor, Robert Dudley, Earl of Leicester.

Penshurst also greatly impressed Elizabeth's successor, King James I. While out hunting one day with his son, Prince Henry, he arrived unannounced. They were pleasantly surprised to find that the absence of the Lady of the house, Sir Robert's wife, Barbara, made no difference to the comforts or hospitality they enjoyed while there. Ben Jonson, another visitor, records the events in his poem, *The Forrest*:

'... and what praise was heaped
On thy goode lady then! who, therein, reaped
The just reward of her high housewifry;
To have her linin, plate and all things nigh
When she was farre; and not a roome but drest
As if it had expected such a guest!'

Recently, in 1986, Penshurst welcomed the Prince of Wales to mark the 400th anniversary of Sir Philip Sidney's death. A year later, HM Queen Elizabeth The Queen Mother was entertained to lunch here, as President of the Victoria Cross and George Cross Association. Her host, the 1st Viscount De L'Isle, was Vice-President of the Association, whose painting of the occasion, by John Worsley, hangs in the Baron's Hall.

29

This painting by John Worsley commemorates the meeting at Penshurst Place in 1987 of the Committee of the Victoria Cross and George Cross Association. The President of the association is HM Queen Elizabeth the Queen Mother and the 1st Viscount De L'Isle was Vice President during his lifetime.

The Sidney Owners of Penshurst

1 *Sir William Sidney (not pictured)*

2 *Sir Henry Sidney*

3 *Sir Philip Sidney*

4 *Robert Sidney, 1st Earl of Leicester*

5 *Robert Sidney, 2nd Earl of Leicester*

6 *Philip Sidney, 3rd Earl of Leicester*

7 *Robert Sidney, 4th Earl of Leicester*

8 *Philip Sidney, 5th Earl of Leicester*

9 *John Sidney, 6th Earl of Leicester*

10 *Jocelyn Sidney, 7th Earl of Leicester*

11 *Elizabeth Perry née Sidney*

12 *Sir John Shelley-Sidney*

13 *Philip Sidney, 1st Lord De L'Isle and Dudley*

14 *Philip Sidney, 2nd Lord De L'Isle and Dudley*

15 *Philip Sidney, 3rd Lord De L'Isle and Dudley*

16 *Algernon Sidney, 4th Lord De L'Isle and Dudley*

17 *William Sidney, 5th Lord De L'Isle and Dudley*

18 *William Sidney, 1st Viscount De L'Isle*

19 *Philip Sidney, 2nd Viscount De L'Isle*

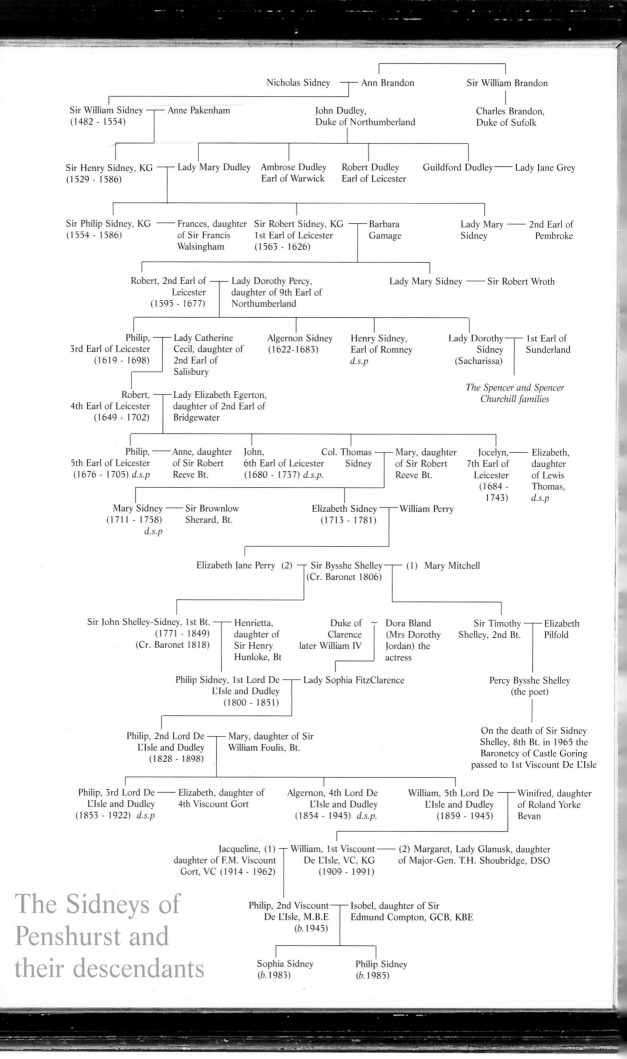

The Sidneys of
Penshurst and
their descendants

A Pictorial view of the House

Two of the life-size carved wooden figures at the base of each of the arched braces.

The BARON'S HALL

The Baron's Hall, built in 1341, is considered to be the best-preserved example of 14th century domestic architecture in England.

The exterior of the Baron's Hall showing the tall gothic arched windows, and to the left, the staircase tower leading to the Solar or State Dining Room.

35

LIFE IN THE BARON'S HALL

Up to the end of the 15th century, Pulteney's hall, or, as it is now known, the Baron's Hall, would at all times have been a mass of people. It was the focal point of the Manor, where those who served it lived out their lives; eating, sleeping and eventually dying there. The family of the house probably slept in the Solar, but would have taken their meals in the hall with everyone else.

The two massive trestle tables on either side of the hall, each measuring over 20ft long, date from this time, and are the only surviving examples of their kind. Here, the servants sat to eat. After meals the tables were taken outside, swilled down with water and propped up against the walls to drain.

The Lord of the Manor and his family sat at a table on the dais at the end of the hall. Guests too, would have enjoyed a seat here, among them several monarchs, including Henry VIII, who was to send the third Duke of Buckingham to his death in 1521, just two years after being so lavishly entertained. Later in that century, the Minstrels' Gallery was added.

The SOLAR or STATE DINING Room

The Solar was the Withdrawing Room of the mediaeval house to which the family would retreat for some privacy or to which the ladies would retire when things got out of hand downstairs.

Originally the room would have been lit from three sides rather than one - the reveals on the west wall and the archway on the north show where the original windows would have been.

38

There is a squint opposite the fireplace - a little window looking down on the Baron's Hall, useful for checking up on what happens below...

The fascinating collection of paintings in the Solar represent influential figures of the 16th and 17th centuries and important members of the Sidney family.

Lady Mary Wroth, daughter of Robert, 1st Earl of Leicester, and wife of Sir Robert Wroth, holding an archlute. English School.

Frances Sidney, née Walsingham, wife of Sir Philip Sidney and their daughter Elizabeth. English School.

Lady Mary Wroth and her mother Barbara, 1st Countess of Leicester, by Marc Gheeraerts.

40

42

The QUEEN ELIZABETH Room

*This room and the next,
the Tapestry Room, are the
first additions to the
original house made by the
Duke of Bedford who lived here
in the early 15th century.*

This is known, rather confusingly, as the
Buckingham building after the Stafford Dukes of
Buckingham who lived here at the end of the 15th
and beginning of the 16th century.

*A 17th century English cabinet
covered with stump work embroidery.*

43

It was built as one large room, a first floor hall
or Great Chamber. The room would have
looked much as the Baron's Hall downstairs.
During Sir Henry Sidney's time as Lord of the
Manor (1554 - 1586) this room was divided
in two and also halved in height by the insertion
of the present ceiling and the building of another
set of rooms above. Queen Elizabeth would have
used it to give audience on one of her many visits.

English 16th century harpsichord in a rococo style, gilded Italian case and mounted on a carved baroque stand.

A portrait of William of Orange hangs beside one of the three rock crystal chandeliers c.1700. It is believed they were given to Henry Sidney, Earl of Romney, by William III.

THE TAPESTRY Room

45

46

Detail of a Gothic tapestry woven in Tournai c.1520.

The PAGES' Room

The small Pages' Room in the corner was where the pages would await summons in the 15th and 16th century.

In the 19th century the room was panelled with shelves to display the family collection of 17th and 18th century oriental porcelain.

*Part of the ornate plaster ceiling
is the Sidney crest of the porcupine.*

The LONG GALLERY

*This wing, completed in 1601, was
built by Sir Robert Sidney and his
wife Barbara Gamage.*

48

Long galleries were very fashionable at the time,
used for taking exercise and showing off portraits,
tapestries and furniture.

*Bronze Death Mask of
Queen Elizabeth I.*

51

The PANELLED Room

This room is the base of one of the defensive towers built at the end of the 14th century and one of eight that surrounded the Baron's Hall.

When constructing the Long Gallery above in the early 17th century, Sir Robert Sidney in effect linked the free-standing tower to the 15th century Buckingham Building. The staircase was built at the same time as the Long Gallery.

A pair of marble busts stand by the window.

The NETHER GALLERY

Sir Philip Sidney's funeral helm is the centrepiece of a fabulous collection of armour and weaponry, much of which has a gruesome, but fascinating history. The 'tassels' on these halberds and pikes were designed to collect the blood dripping from the blades during battle.

53

Detail of a German executioner's sword showing an engraving of a man hanging at the gallows.

Detail of a finely engraved helm.

Detail of the hilt of Robert Dudley, Earl of Leicester's Sword of State.

The Gardens
& Park

55

Gardening on the grand scale

*We have set out to create a garden for all seasons…
and have gone some way to achieve that end.*

William, 1st Viscount De L'Isle VC KG

The village of Penshurst guards the secret of the
great house at its heart. The little high street, with
its cluster of shops and houses, hardly permits as
much as a glimpse of the high pitched roofs of the
mediaeval hall or the ancient chimneys of Penshurst
Place which stand so close behind them. Through
the entrance arch from the road, the run of
Elizabethan wall and high yew hedge hide, though
hint at, the sight behind. Yet even that hint cannot
fully prepare the visitor for all that lies beyond.
The garden is one of the oldest in private
ownership, and few others can be traced back so
far. The earliest records are dated 1346, and show
that it has been here at least since the time of
Pulteney's hall. The intervening centuries have
inevitably brought their own changes – but a good
deal fewer than to most other gardens of note. A
large part of the Penshurst garden today has the
rare privilege of remaining as it was constructed in
the reign of Queen Elizabeth I.

Like a bright gem, the garden appears all the more
remarkable in the green ring of its setting. The
estate woods, parkland and dateless landscape rising
around it, accentuate both its formality and its
cosiness. Though an unlikely combination, the
garden has both qualities. The geometry of the mile
of yew hedge criss-crossing much of its 11 acres
creates a series of small garden rooms, each neatly
self-contained and presenting its own private

delights. Lying to the south-east, this pattern of small gardens opens out directly in front of the house into the 16th century Italian Garden, the view of which is designed to be enjoyed from the state rooms. The colossal project of Sir Henry Sidney in the 1560's, it is the centrepiece of the garden and sets the style for the whole.

Henry wanted to create a garden on a scale befitting the huge defensive system of walls and towers built in the late 14th century by Sir John Devereux, but in the 16th century style. However, it required a large area of flat ground, which the garden did not have. So Henry embarked on the ambitious task of remoulding the contours of the land in front of the house, adjusting the natural lie to the south-east of the ground and creating a multi-level area measuring 360 x 300ft (110 x 91.5m). The scheme involved shifting thousands of tons of earth and building an ingenious system of walls and terraces. A garden to supply fruit and vegetables for the house was made on a lower level. Today, visitors to Penshurst Place may still appreciate the achievements of Sir Henry Sidney, his work having remained virtually unaltered for 400 years. A more immediate beneficiary, however, was his son, Sir Robert, who inherited not only Penshurst but much of his father's interest in its garden. He completed the walling of the orchard, the framework of which remains to this day and, as letters to and from his servants at Penshurst suggest, he was keenly concerned with its development.

Among other fruits, apricots and peaches were grown. A letter written from London to Thomas Golding at the estate in April 1605 shows that frost was a worry: *"I have receaved your letter and thogh that at the wryting of it the frosts had don no hurt to the appricottes and peaches yet they which have come since I feare have spoiled all...I would be glad*

once more to know how they are." A later note on the carrying out of Robert's instructions on new planting, written to him from the estate in 1611, shows him to have been as keen as ever to see exotic fruit at Penshurst. The report reads: *"There were 4 peache trees grafted, 3 plumme trees, 3 peare trees and 2 apples...The peaches are disposed into severall places where wee thought fittest."*

57

Fruit was still a preoccupation over a century later, when Jocelyn, 7th Earl of Leicester, had charge of Penshurst and its garden. In view of his reputation for living life on the wild side, his desire to obtain good grafts of cider apples is hardly surprising. Records show that the varieties *Red Streak* and *Nonpareil* were grown, the latter still to be found in the orchard today. By 1744 Penshurst was in the hands of William Perry, another of its less celebrated custodians. A gardener was brought in to plant, at his own expense, thousands of yards of Dutch box, roses and *"40 or so pretty curiosities"*, while orange trees and other exotics arrived from various garden suppliers. However, Perry was more enthusiastic about his garden than about paying his bills, as those he employed were to discover to their cost. After he was interned in an asylum, his widow Elizabeth (formerly Elizabeth Sidney) maintained the garden on a chiefly utilitarian basis, and in the

latter years of the century, managed by trustees, it drifted into a state of naturalistic disorder.

Writing in 1810, a local historian noted: *"The gardens still retain their original form of terraces and multibank divisions but these are neglected and indeed form a perfect wilderness."* Yet while the Penshurst incumbents' lack of funds was to some extent the ruin of the garden, it was also its rescue inasmuch as it did retain its terraces. Had the money been available, they might well have been swept away by the 18th century fashion for landscaped parkland that overtook so many country house gardens.

The 19th century renaissance of the garden at Penshurst was due in no small way to Philip, 1st Lord De L'Isle and Dudley, and one Mr Bridger, who was taken on in 1820 as Head Gardener and remained in the post for the next 48 years. Philip's good work was continued by his son, also Philip, who inherited Penshurst in 1851 as 2nd Lord De L'Isle and Dudley, and who wanted to revive the

traditions of formality in garden design, using the pattern of his ancestor's scheme as his guide. Those who have followed him at Penshurst have been equally sensitive in their work, any changes growing naturally within his framework. The rejuvenation of the Italian Garden, central to Philip's programme, was his most impressive project. Four panels were laid to form a rectangle on the level plat, slightly sunk for visual emphasis, and separated by broad gravel paths. Each of these quarters was sub-divided into six box-hedged beds which, every spring and summer, came alive with the blooms of perennials and annuals. In the centre was placed a lily pond, formed as an oval to appear as a perfect circle when seen from the house, and surmounted by a fountain and classical statue.

Meanwhile, to the east of the Italian Garden, a jigsaw of rectangular garden rooms was created by the planting of a great network of high, clipped yew hedges, which still remain. Colour and variety was lent to the little gardens by the bedding out of annuals. Today, the grass paths which lead from one to the other take the visitor from a rose garden

59

60

to a magnolia garden, from an apple orchard to a nut garden, from a great floral Union Flag to a small grass amphitheatre.

In Philip's time, most of the borders featured an edging of carnations. In 1868 the redoubtable Mr Bridger had handed over the Head Gardener reins to his son Frederick, who was himself to serve for 65 years at Penshurst, and who was a noted carnation grower. A yellow *malmaison* carnation he raised was awarded a first-class certificate by the Royal Horticultural Society in 1885. He named it *Pride of Penshurst*. Across his entire garden, Philip ran two main pathways, one going north from the wrought iron garden gate, the other running from the west, and which still add to the enjoyment of the garden today. From various points along these walks the visitor is presented with foliage-framed

views of the house or of the distant rise of the Penshurst countryside.

By the start of the 20th century the gardens at Penshurst had come to be recognised as the perfect example of the old English style, their fame spreading far and wide. But another period of decay was around the corner. During the Second World War Algernon, 4th Lord De L'Isle and Dudley, was obliged to leave the estate as a result of enemy action during the winter of 1944/5. His enforced absence and the lack of available labour allowed only a minimum of caretaking, and all that could be managed was the trimming of the yew hedges and the pruning of the fruit trees. Beneath them, the weeds once again began to take hold.

Photo: David Sellman

Forget me not

We went to see Penshurst, famous for its gardens and excellent fruit.

John Evelyn, 1652

"Hedges and apple trees apart, I think we can say that everything that now grows in these gardens represents a portion of the effort we have made to restore them to their former elegance and beauty." Such were the reflections in 1990 of William, 1st Viscount De L'Isle on almost 45 years of work on the gardens at Penshurst following their decline during the war. Thanks to some expert fruit tree pruning and regular clipping of the yew hedges during the war years, the orchards and wall fruit had been kept in good shape, and the main framework of the garden remained. However, all the floral achievements of William's grandfather, Philip, 2nd Lord De L'Isle and Dudley, had been strangled by weeds and the lawns had reverted to pasture.

Thus, when the new family settled into Penshurst in the autumn of 1945 a large motor mower found itself near the top of the shopping list. It was put to work after the worst of the rough grass had been burned off, the blaze so fierce that it was mistaken by neighbours for a great fire in the house itself. The Italian Garden demanded immediate attention too. All the box hedges were grubbed and the ground elder which infested the beds poisoned. Floribunda roses were planted. The major work, however, was to revive and develop the old yew enclosures to the east. Lord and Lady De L'Isle also wanted to add to them and there was a ready-made opportunity to do so. At the time, the kitchen garden occupied about half of the entire garden within the walls, and abutted on the section of garden rooms. But as the problem of food shortages receded so market gardening became less important, and new enclosures could easily be extended into the kitchen area – which also conveniently offered a yew hedge network planted to conceal greenhouses.

Today, these little rooms form the greater part of the garden, offering an abundance of variety in form, foliage and bloom, and ensuring continuous displays from spring to autumn. They have drawn

Photo: David Sellman

extensively on the treasury of plants now available and on the skills of some of the country's leading garden designers. Their development continues. At the old garden gate, the visitor is flanked by two broad herbaceous borders along the main path running north towards the house. He is in the midst of the scheme of garden rooms but as yet they are unseen, tucked away behind the borders on either side – great runs of banked colour designed to provide a sense of anticipation, with their abundance of iris and foxglove, lupin and astilbe, geum and forget-me-not, lily, achillea and many more.

Photo: David Sellman

To the far west, or left of the visitor, is the Italian Garden. In-between lie two of the larger hedged enclosures, the Rose Garden and, to its north, the Spring and Autumn Garden. In the latter, nut and apple trees are underplanted with daffodils, whilst late summer and autumn perennials fill the beds. Linking the Rose and Spring and Autumn Gardens is an east-west mixed border, again designed to provide continuous interest. Created by Lanning Roper in the 1970s, the garden is named after him. To the right of the main path from the entrance gates lies the larger part of the patchwork of garden rooms. This is bordered to the south by a stunning 100metre bed of peonies, a broad carmine ribbon of bloom in June streaming away to the east. Immediately above it stands the old orchard of apple trees, pruned during the war years into the correct umbrella shape for picking. *"The resulting architectural shape is now a particular feature of the whole garden,"* the 1st Viscount De L'Isle was to note towards the end of his life, *"and in May we are submerged under a sea of apple blossom."*

More recently, the garden at Penshurst has been described as *"a homage to the apple tree"*. As part of William's extensive reshaping work, one corner of the orchard was removed in the early 1970s in favour of a new plantation of Kentish cobs and crab apples, designed by John Codrington. Through the trees in this Nut Garden a grass path leads from each corner to a green open space where clematis, roses and honeysuckle swathe a pergola. In spring, the grass is alive with daffodils, primroses and tulips, followed by bluebells and marguerites.

Also designed by John Codrington are the Magnolia Garden and Grey Garden, both to the north of the orchard. Removing old glasshouses made way for the first, several varieties of magnolia being planted in the resulting sunken area. Its centrepiece is a sculpture of a naiad, erected to the memory of the 1st Viscount De L'Isle's first wife, Jacqueline. It was completed in 1991, just a month before his own death. In the Grey Garden, on the site of the old bonfire yard, fruit trees add height and perspective to the main area of brick paving, spotted with low, spreading plantings of grey, white and silver. These include artemesia, pyrus, achillea, anthemis,

65

66

dianthus, stachys and white roses. Separating these two Codrington designs is the Stage Garden, in the area formerly used for drying laundry. This pastoral theatre, used for open air performances, comprises a semi-circular grass stage facing an auditorium.

The last major project of Lord De L'Isle represented the fulfilment of a long-held ambition. In 1984 work was begun on the restitution of a Union Flag Garden, which had been a feature of the 19th century enclosure where today's Rose Garden thrives. It is set in two acres in the north-east corner, flanked by hedge and garden wall, the flag depicted in the colours of fragrant lavender, roses and red and white tulips. The grand design of the flag can be fully appreciated from the rose-smothered viewing platform. On the completion of the Union Flag Garden, a mulberry tree was planted by HRH Prince of Wales to mark the 400th anniversary of Sir Philip Sidney's death.

The evolution of the garden at Penshurst is continuous. Its current custodians, Philip, 2nd Viscount De L'Isle and his wife, Isobel, believe in horticultural change – that a garden should always be fresh and surprising. And like those who were here before them, they are making their mark. New work is determined by the existing structure of the garden, which also requires constant attention, and restoration of three of the garden's ponds was

Photo: David Markson

amongst Lord and Lady De L'Isle's first achievements. Chief among them is Diana's Bath, refurbished in 1890 from a Tudor stew pond supplying fish for the household and water for the garden. The pond, which lies to the south-west of the Union Flag, was drained and cleared of mud and silt, and the walls were re-rendered. Planting in many areas of the garden has been renewed with modern varieties, integrated with forms that have been grown for centuries.

Every year the mile of yew hedges must be clipped and shaped. Three thousand roses need pruning, spraying and dead-heading. Constant care is demanded by the trees: the 450-year-old yew in the south-west corner of the Italian Garden; the century-old Ginkgo biloba, with its maidenhair fern leaves, gracing the Long Gallery; the 18th century lime avenue flanking the northern edge of the garden; the avenue of beech, sweet chestnut and oak in the park known as *Sacharissa's Walk*. And storms, of course, add to the workload.

The Penshurst estate has long been the guardian, too, of Sidney's Oak. Reputed to have been planted at the christening of Sir Philip Sidney in 1554, it is, in fact, 1,000 years old. Now its great age is telling and it cannot survive much longer, but its acorns have been planted around the world, the 1st Viscount De L'Isle always carrying a handful with him on his travels. Meanwhile, others are driving roots into the soil of Penshurst's own gardens and park. Continuity of life for the oak of Norman Conquest times has also now been assured by 21st century science. As a result of cloning, saplings genetically identical to the tree are to be planted on the estate. The establishment here of generations of Sidney's Oak is, it seems, as assured as that of the Sidneys themselves.

69

The Toy Museum

In addition to their tour of the house and gardens, visitors to Penshurst Place should not miss the opportunity to visit The Toy Museum.

The collection includes toys played with and enjoyed by generations of Sidneys, while many once belonged to Yootha Rose, stage designer, artist and toymaker, and an avid collector of toys. Numerous others have been given or lent to Lord De L'Isle for the collection.

70

Photo: David Markson

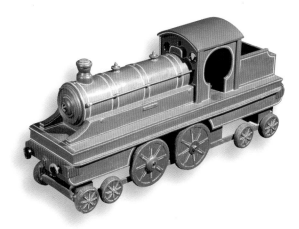

Photo:
David
Markson

The displays form a veritable treasure trove of dolls and dolls' houses, teddies, soldiers, mechanical toys and general playthings, mostly from the Victorian and Edwardian eras. From an earlier period, though, is Moggie, a Georgian doll made between 1750 and 1800 and loved by generations of children from one Kentish family. Her head and torso are carved from a single block of wood covered with gesso and painted.

Look out, too, for the toy theatre and its little paper actors, the straw Noah's Ark complete with wooden animals made by French prisoners of war in the early 19th century, and the big bear – put your money in and watch his eyes light up as he takes a drink!

The museum was opened in July 1970. It was created within an old carpenters' workshop, and is part of a range of "Gothic" stables of 1836, built by the current Lord De L'Isle's great-great-grandfather.

71

PENSHURST PLACE
AND GARDENS

The garden at Penshurst is of the same age as the original building – over six hundred years. This makes it one of the oldest gardens in private ownership in Britain.

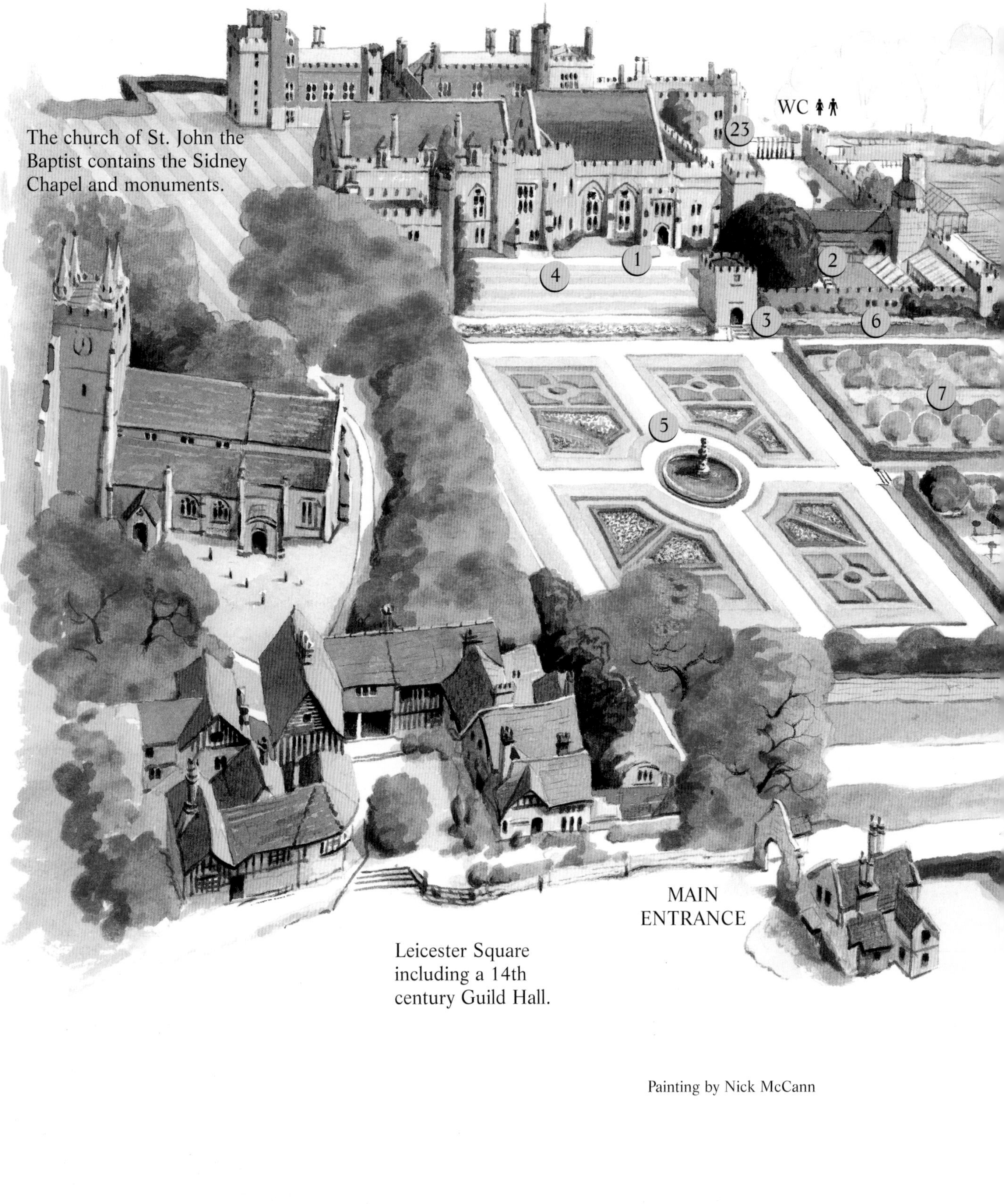

The church of St. John the Baptist contains the Sidney Chapel and monuments.

WC ♀♂

23

4

1

2

3

6

7

5

MAIN ENTRANCE

Leicester Square including a 14th century Guild Hall.

Painting by Nick McCann